Portage Public Library

DISCARDED

The Pheasant

First Steck-Vaughn Edition 1992

This book has been reviewed
for accuracy by
David Skryja
Associate Professor of Biology
University of Wisconsin Center—Waukesha.

Library of Congress Cataloging in Publication Data

Endo, Kimio.
　The pheasant.

　(Nature close-ups)
　Translation of: Kiji no kurashi / photographs and
text by Kimio Endō.
　Summary: Text and photographs describe the life
cycle, behavior, and natural habitat of the pheasant.
　1. Pheasants—Juvenile literature.　[1. Pheasants]
I. Title.　II. Series.
QL696.G27E4413　1986　　598'.617　　85-28207

ISBN 0-8172-2549-8 (lib. bdg.)
ISBN 0-8172-2574-9 (softcover)

This edition first published in 1986 by Raintree Publishers Limited Partnership, a Division of Steck-Vaughn Company.

Text copyright © 1986 by Raintree Publishers Limited Partnership, translated by Jun Amano from *Pheasant* copyright © 1982 by Kimio Endo.

Photographs copyright © 1982 by Kimio Endo.

World English translation rights for *Color Photo Books on Nature* arranged with Kaisei-Sha through Japan Foreign-Rights Center.

All rights reserved. No part of the material protected by this copyright may be reproduced or utilized in any form by any means, electronic or mechanical, including photocopying, recording, or by any information storage and retrieval system, without permission in writing from Steck-Vaughn Company, P.O. Box 26015, Austin, TX 78755. Printed in the United States of America.

3 4 5 6 7 8 9 0　　　　95 94 93 92

The Pheasant

◀ An area in Japan where pheasants live.

Pheasants prefer grassy areas with low shrubs and bushes, which offer protection.

▶ A pheasant in an orchard in springtime.

The tall grass in this orchard provides good nesting sites for the females. And the trees offer a place for the pheasants to roost at night.

Although the ring-necked pheasant is now fairly common in the United States, at one time there weren't any pheasants at all in North America. Pheasants originated in the Asian countries, the ring-necks from China, and other kinds, or species, from Korea and Japan. Gradually, the beautiful and tasty game birds were introduced to other parts of the world. And in the late 1800s, a small flock was shipped to Oregon where they soon began to thrive in their new homeland. Although their colors vary, the nesting and feeding habits of most pheasants are similar. The pheasant featured in this book has been named the national bird of Japan.

◀ A male (right) and female (left).

While the bright colors of the males vary from species to species, female pheasants are usually a buff brown and rather dull-looking in comparison.

◀ **A male surveying his territory.**

The male climbs to the top of a hill to survey his territory. Then he crows over and over again to warn other males in the area that he has claimed this land for his own.

In early March, the male pheasant, or cock, leaves the flock of birds with which he has lived during the winter and sets out on his own. He searches for a suitable place to live during the coming months. He looks for an area that has tall grasses and low shrubs and trees. These areas provide protection from enemies and are also good nesting sites for his mates. He also looks for adequate supplies of food and water. When he has found a suitable place, the cock crows loudly over and over again to let other pheasants in the area know that this is his territory.

● **Two males fighting over territory (photos 1-4).**

If two birds try to claim the same territory, they may fight each other. But usually the stronger male can frighten the weaker one by making a showy display of its feathers. If the two birds do actually fight, they peck with their strong beaks and beat their wings at one another.

● The cock struts and displays his showy feathers as he tries to attract a female (photos 1-6).

While the cock has been loudly proclaiming his territory to other males, the females, or hens, in the area have also heard his cries. In April, he starts to court them, one at a time. He begins by showing off, turning his head from side to side. As he does so, the red skin patches on his head and cheeks turn a brighter red. He struts closer to the female and turns in a circle to display himself, with his colorful breast feathers gleaming in the sun. Then he spreads his plumed tail and wings, ruffling his feathers so that he almost doubles in size. He does all of this to impress the female so that she will be his mate and live in his territory.

▶ The male's crowing has attracted two females.

The male puffs himself up as he begins to show off his beautiful feathers for these hens.

◀ **A male's colorful head and neck feathers.**

The red patches on the cock's head and cheeks get even brighter red when he is trying to attract a mate, or scare off an enemy.

▶ **A male showing a female where to find food.**

This male's colorful feathers are still fully displayed as he approaches the female and invites her to feed with him.

After he has completed his colorful display, the male makes a clucking noise, inviting the female to feed with him. He shows her some seeds, or a flower bud, or other food that is nearby. If she eats the food, he knows she has accepted his invitation to nest in his territory. The two pheasants will mate several times during the next few weeks.

The male goes through this same courting ritual with other hens. He may choose as many as four mates to live in his territory.

▶ **A male pheasant displaying his feathers (photos 1-2).**

The male ruffles his feathers so that he seems to be almost twice his real size.

◀ **A female looking for a nest site.**

The hen pheasant looks for a good place to make her nest. She may test several spots before building the nest.

The female pheasant makes her nest on the ground. She searches for a place well hidden in the grass or beneath shrubs. She may test several nest sites before she makes her final choice. Meanwhile, the male stands guard, watching and listening for danger.

The hen lays one light brown egg a day, from six to sixteen eggs in all. Then she begins to incubate them—she sits on them to keep them warm. The hen incubates her eggs for twenty-two to twenty-four days before they hatch. Meanwhile, the male stands by, guarding the nest.

▶ **A hen turning over her eggs.**

The hen uses her beak to turn her eggs once a day. Perhaps she turns them to ensure that they will be warmed on all sides.

▶ **A fox looking for prey.**

Foxes are enemies of pheasants and try to steal eggs from their nests.

▼ **A pheasant nest with eggs.**

The hen's nest is made of leaves and dried grasses and is well hidden by shrubs. Foxes, raccoons, and snakes all prey upon pheasants' eggs.

◀ **Newly hatched chicks.**

It may take six to twelve hours for all the chicks in the nest to hatch. When they are first hatched, their down is wet. The chicks stay warm by huddling beneath their mother's wings.

▶ **A hen pheasant and her chicks.**

The hen clucks to her chicks constantly, "talking" to them. They cheep in response, and she can always tell where they are in the tall grass.

In late May or early June, the eggs begin to hatch. Each baby chick uses a bump on its beak, called an egg tooth, to crack its shell. Then the chick wriggles and squirms until it breaks free of the shell.

The tiny baby chicks are covered with brown and yellow down which blends in well with their surroundings. This camouflage helps keep them safe from enemies such as bobcats, raccoons, and foxes.

◀ **A baby chick's egg tooth.**

The egg tooth will disappear about three days after the chick has hatched from the egg.

◀ A chick looking for food.

Pheasants will eat almost any insect they can find, but caterpillars, spiders, and young crickets are among their favorite foods.

▶ Pheasants sand-bathing.

Pheasants do not bathe in water, but they often take sand baths and play in the sand.

As is true of all animals, baby pheasants are born knowing many things instinctively. But the chicks still have a lot to learn from watching their mother. The first thing she does is to show them where to look for food. Pheasants eat a variety of things, including berries, fruits, seeds, and grains, but most of those are not ripe until fall. So the hen leads her chicks to a place where there are a lot of insects. She shows the chicks how to scratch and peck the ground for ants, beetles, bugs and worms.

▶ Pheasants scratching for food.

The hen pheasant shows the chicks how to scratch and peck for food. Barnyard chickens look for insects in the same way.

◀ **A hen pheasant trying to drive off crows.**

The hen beats her wings fiercely, trying to drive away these crows which threaten her chicks.

Many animals hunt, or prey upon, pheasants, including cats and dogs, skunks, raccoons, hawks, and owls. With so many enemies, the chicks' lives are constantly in danger. If the chicks are threatened by a predator, the hen will try to protect them. She may pretend she has a broken wing or leg. She will flutter about, trying to draw the predator's attention away from her chicks, giving them time to escape. As a last resort, she may attack the enemy, beating at it with her strong wings and pecking with her hard beak.

▶ **A mother crow and her babies.**

This mother crow shares portions of a dead pheasant chick with her own babies. As pheasants grow older, they are able to run faster to escape crows. But when they are newly hatched, the chicks are in great danger of being eaten.

◀ **A male cries out when danger comes near.**

If a male pheasant senses an enemy approaching, he gives a loud cry of warning.

▼ **Baby chicks hiding in the grass.**

Their brown and yellow coloring helps young chicks to blend in with dried grasses and leaves, keeping them hidden from enemies.

◄ **A hen and her chicks in the rain.**

Even in the rain, pheasants hunt for food. It is easy to find earthworms and grubs because the rain brings them out.

▶ **A baby pheasant learning to fly.**

This baby chick is trying to fly. When one chick has learned to fly, the others will try to imitate it.

◄ **Baby pheasants under their mother's wings.**

The chicks rest under their mother's wings in cold weather, and beside her when the weather is nice.

Young pheasants eat almost constantly. They must consume almost their entire body weight in food each day if they are to grow to full size by the end of summer.

By the time the young pheasants are five weeks old, their baby down has disappeared. It has been replaced by a full coat of brown baby feathers. Once their wing feathers are developed, the young pheasants learn how to fly, usually by trial and error. With the help of a strong wind, they are soon able to fly short distances.

◄ **Pheasant chicks grooming themselves.**

Like other birds, pheasants spend a lot of time grooming themselves. They secrete an oily liquid and rub it on their wings to waterproof them.

◀ **Pheasants eating snake eggs.**

Snakes are the enemies of pheasant eggs and chicks, but adult pheasants, in turn, feed on snake eggs.

▶ **A pheasant eating grass seed.**

This young male is eating grass seeds. Pheasants that live near farms may also feed on wheat, barley, and corn kernels left over from harvesting.

By the time the chicks are six weeks old, they have shed their baby feathers and begun to grow adult feathers. As this final set of feathers is growing, it is possible to tell the males from the females, for the first time. The male's neck and breast feathers are bright and colorful, while the female's are a dull brown. Red patches begin to develop on the male's face and cheeks, and his voice changes.

As the summer wears on, the pheasants can find fruits, berries, and seeds to supplement their diet.

▶ **A young pheasant beginning to grow adult feathers.**

This young cock's red face patches have developed, and its shoulder and breast feathers are brightly colored. Eventually, the young male will also grow long tail plumes.

▼ **A male (left) and female pheasant.** These young pheasants are almost fully grown. They are well camouflaged because their colors blend so well with their surroundings.

▶ **A young male pheasant.**

This young male pheasant is almost ready to leave his mother and begin exploring new territory by himself. Sometimes young cocks will challenge one another when they have matured to this stage.

It is late September or early October before the young hens and cocks have grown all of their feathers. Because their colors blend in well with their surroundings, they are well-hidden from predators. As the young male matures, he begins to wander off on his own to explore new territory. But he does not stray far. Unlike some birds, which fly south for the winter, pheasants live in the same general area all year.

Autumn is an especially dangerous time for pheasants because of the fall hunting season. Most male pheasants live only two or three years. Hens may live a year longer, since they are not usually hunted.

▶ **Berries and fruits in autumn.**

In the fall, berries and seeds are plentiful. Pheasants perch on the branches of trees to eat berries like these.

◀ **A field in late fall.**

A group of pheasants bands together in this field. Now fully grown, the young pheasants look just like the adults. It is impossible to tell them apart.

▶ **A pheasant in flight.**

If a pheasant is startled by a hunting dog or a group of hunters, it will fly away in order to escape. But pheasants can only fly short distances.

Pheasants live only in certain parts of the world. They do not live in deserts or dense forests because they could not find sufficient food there. They prefer areas where the temperatures are somewhat mild and where there are plenty of grain fields, grasslands, and low shrubs. There are many pheasants in southern Canada, in the northern United States, in parts of Europe, and, of course, in their Asian homeland.

▶ **A male pheasant running.**

Pheasants have well-developed legs and can run as fast as hunting dogs when they are being chased. They often run to thickets or shrubs for cover.

◄ **A male pheasant in winter.**

The male's face becomes paler in winter and his wing colors lose some of their brightness.

By late fall, pheasants begin to band together for the winter. The males no longer challenge each other or fight with one another. No courting or mating takes place. Young and old, male and female, all flock together for safety, making it more difficult for predators to attack them.

Because of their many layers of feathers, pheasants can withstand cold weather fairly well. And, like most animals, they can live for a long time on stored fat. The older birds in the flock show the younger birds where to look for food beneath the snow.

◄ **Pheasants foraging for food.**

Pheasants search for dried grasses and seeds in the winter. Here, they look for food near a river.

▶ **A pheasant in the snow.**

Pheasants hide under bushes or roost in trees during heavy snowstorms.

◀ **Pheasants searching for food in early spring.**

The pheasants search for food in places where the sun has melted the snow. They look for berries or fresh new green buds and leaves.

▶ **Pheasants pecking for food.**

Sometimes in the spring, pheasants will peck and scratch for the roots of grasses, leaving holes in fields. But generally pheasants are helpful to farmers because they eat harmful insects and weed seeds.

But winter is a dangerous time for pheasants. Many of the older, weaker birds do not survive the cold weather. Others fall prey to hawks, owls, and other hungry predators. Some of the pheasants will smother in huge snowdrifts. Also, if ice forms a crust on the snow, the birds may not be able to forage for food. Only the smartest and strongest of the pheasants live through the winter.

When spring comes, the young males that have survived the cold weather leave the flock. They wander off on their own, in search of territories to claim and hens to court.

GLOSSARY

camouflage—to hide by blending with the environment. (pp. 15, 24)

cock—an adult male pheasant. (pp. 6, 8, 25)

down—a newborn chick's soft, fluffy covering of feathers. (p. 15)

egg tooth—a bump on the baby pheasant's beak, which is used to crack the eggshell. (p. 15)

hen—an adult female pheasant. (p. 8)

incubate—to sit on eggs to keep them warm so they will hatch. (p. 12)

instinct—behavior with which an animal is born, rather than behavior which is learned. (p. 16)

predators—animals which hunt and kill other animals for food. (pp. 18, 25)

prey—animals that are killed by predators. (p. 13)

species—a group of animals which scientists have identified as having common traits. (p. 4)

territory—an area that a male pheasant claims for himself and his hens. (pp. 6, 8, 10)